Protecting Sea Turtles

by Amy Edgar illustrated by Tom Leonard

HOUGHTON MIFFLIN BOSTON

INTRODUCING SEA TURTLES

Sea turtles have lived on Earth since the days of the dinosaurs. But now these turtles are threatened.

Three Kinds of Sea Turtles

Hawksbill Kemp's Ridley Loggerhead

There are seven kinds of sea turtles, and all of them are endangered. The Kemp's Ridley sea turtle is in the most danger. In 1947, 40,000 Kemp's Ridley sea turtles laid eggs in one day. In 1998, only 2,000 of them laid eggs in the whole year! Scientists fear that these turtles are in danger of extinction. Kemp's Ridley sea turtles may disappear from the oceans forever.

Why are so few sea turtles left? One answer is that people have harmed the turtles and the places where they live.

FEATURES OF SEA TURTLES

Sea turtles and land turtles are different in some important ways. A land turtle can pull its head inside its shell to hide from danger. A sea turtle cannot do this. When there is danger, a sea turtle swims away. A sea turtle has flippers for swimming. A land turtle has feet and claws for walking.

land turtle

Kemp's Ridley

Sea turtles are the fastest swimmers of all the four-legged animals. Some sea turtles can swim 20 miles per hour. A sea turtle has flippers that are shaped like paddles. It swims by flapping its two front flippers like wings. The back flippers are used to help the sea turtle go left or right.

The Kemp's Ridley sea turtle is about two feet long, with a dark green-gray shell and skin. It is smaller than other sea turtles, usually weighing about 100 pounds. In comparison, the Leatherback sea turtle usually weighs about 1,000 pounds.

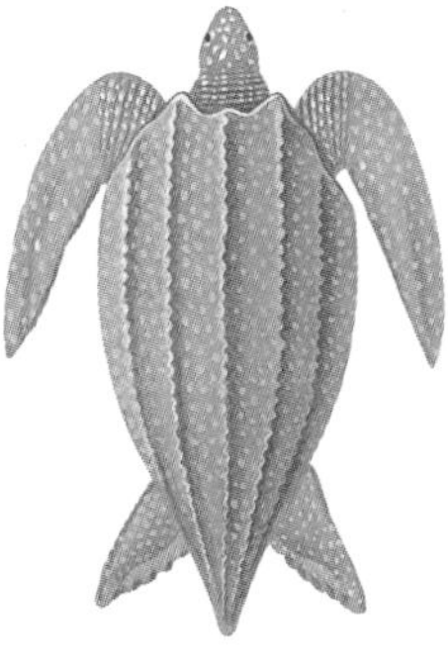

Leatherback

Kemp's Ridley

Sea turtles need to breathe air. Active turtles swim to the surface of the water often for a breath of air. They take in oxygen from the air they breathe. That helps them stay underwater for a long time. When it is time for a turtle to sleep, it sinks to the bottom of the ocean. The water is colder there, so the turtle needs less oxygen to breathe. Resting turtles stay underwater for up to two hours.

Sea turtles can't chew food because they don't have teeth. But sea turtles have very strong jaws, and they use their jaws to crush fish to eat. They can even crush hard clam shells. Fish and jellyfish are two of their favorite foods.

Sea turtles live in the ocean. But the female sea turtle returns to land to lay her eggs.

A SEA TURTLE RETURNS TO LAND

A female Kemp's Ridley sea turtle is graceful in the water but slow on land. To move on land, she must drag herself over sand with her flippers. That's probably why she doesn't return to land until she has to lay her eggs. The sea turtle looks for a place on the beach high enough to protect her eggs from the tide coming in. When she finds a safe place, she uses her back flippers to dig a hole in the sand.

When the hole is deep enough, the sea turtle starts to lay her eggs. She drops the soft, round eggs into the hole, one by one. Then the sea turtle covers the eggs with sand. She slowly drags herself back to the sea and swims away.

The eggs hatch in about fifty days. Sea turtle babies don't see their mothers. They are born knowing how to swim and they can find their way into the ocean. But it's not always easy for them to stay alive.

THE STRUGGLE TO SURVIVE

Sea turtles are threatened by people in different ways. Shrimp boats use large nets to catch shrimp. The nets sometimes catch sea turtles too. Some people hunt sea turtles for their skin, shells, and meat. People still make wallets, jewelry, and soup from sea turtles.

People who live near beaches can be a danger to sea turtles. As people play on the beach, they may accidentally crush turtle eggs. Sea turtles can also swallow things that people throw away, such as plastic bags. A plastic bag may look like a jellyfish to a turtle. The plastic can choke the sea turtle, or it can keep the turtle floating on the surface of the water, unable to dive for food.

PROTECTING SEA TURTLES

Some people are taking action to protect sea turtles. They want fishermen to use an invention called a Turtle Excluding Device (TED). The TED lets the turtle escape from the fisherman's net. But sadly, many fishermen won't use the TED when they fish for shrimp.

The fishermen who do not use the nets say they cost too much and are difficult to use.

Other people are trying to protect turtles on the beaches. A hotel in Palm Beach, Florida, built a special walkway to the beach so that people will not walk on turtle eggs in the sand.

SCIENTISTS WANT TO HELP

Scientists and volunteers are working to protect sea turtles. They are finding ways to protect the turtle eggs and the baby turtles. One way to protect them is to move the eggs to a laboratory until the baby turtles hatch.

Volunteers go to the beach and look for places where a sea turtle could have left her eggs. A volunteer who finds turtle tracks shows the tracks to the scientist. This helps the scientist find the eggs.

The scientist digs up the turtle eggs. The eggs are counted and put into a box with sand from the nest. The sand may help the turtles come back to the same beach.

The scientist takes notes on the number of eggs, how deep the nest is, the time of day, and the weather. The nesting place is then marked with a pole. The scientist will bring the baby turtles back to the nesting place when they are ready to go into the sea.

AT THE LABORATORY

The scientist takes the eggs back to the laboratory. There the eggs are put in a hole like the one their mother made for them at the beach. Now the scientist waits for about fifty days for the baby turtles to hatch. The eggs are not allowed to get too hot or too cold.

As the turtles start hatching and moving about in the nesting hole, they work together to dig their way out. The scientist counts and weighs the babies. Then the scientist and the volunteers go back to the beach where they found the eggs.

BACK ON THE BEACH

At the beach, the baby turtles come out of their box. Volunteers watch them carefully and chase away birds and crabs. These animals like to eat baby turtles. When a baby turtle goes the wrong way, a volunteer carefully puts it in the water. The baby swims away to begin its new life in the ocean.

A baby turtle's life is difficult. Baby sea turtles may be eaten by a fish or a crab, or they may eat a plastic top from a bottle. Fish nets may catch them. Scientists believe that only one out of every hundred babies lives to be an adult turtle.

PROTECTING THE KEMP'S RIDLEY SEA TURTLE

Scientists hope that protecting the Kemp's Ridley sea turtle eggs will help more babies to survive. They want to increase the number of these turtles. They hope that when the baby turtles become adults they will come back to lay eggs.

The Kemp's Ridley sea turtle is still endangered. But scientists have reason for hope. In recent years, the number of turtle nests found in Texas and Mexico has increased. In 1995, only four nests were found on Padre Island. In 1998, thirteen nests were found there.

Will the sea turtle survive in our world? We can only help them and hope they will.